# The
# PROTEA
## family in Southern Africa

Colin Paterson-Jones

# CONTENTS

# INTRODUCTION

A line drawn across the map of Africa from the Kunene River in the west to the Zambezi in the east demarcates (somewhat arbitrarily) the region known as southern Africa, a subcontinent well known for its scenic beauty. This reputation derives, at least in part, from its huge variety of landscapes. This is indeed a land of contrasts: the fynbos-clad mountains of the Western Cape could not be more different from the sun-scorched plains of the Namib Desert less than 1 000 km to the north; the arid inland plateau of the Great Karoo stands in stark counterpoint to the lush, tropical and subtropical eastern coastal hinterland.

What is not so well known, though, is the enormous wealth of living things that occur here naturally, a biodiversity which is a direct consequence of this extraordinary range of habitats.

Understandably, perhaps, southern Africa's large animals command the most attention (its game parks attract millions of visitors each year), but in truth an even greater natural treasure is the region's unique plant-life. How many people realise that South Africa alone contains two of the world's internationally recognized biological 'hot-spots' – the Cape Floral Region, and the Succulent Karoo of Namaqualand and the Little Karoo? What sets these areas of exceptional natural riches apart from anything found elsewhere is not their animals but, as their names suggest, their plants. The Cape and Succulent Karoo floras are not only unique but many of their component plants are especially beautiful.

This book is a showcase for one of the subcontinent's most charismatic groups of plants: the protea family, known botanically as the Proteaceae. Members of this family are found over a large area in this region but are absent from the vast expanses of desert and semidesert. They are seen in its most splendid variety in the fynbos, the dominant vegetation type of the Cape flora. Indeed, the Proteaceae is one of the three characteristic fynbos families, the other two being the Cape reeds (Restionaceae) and the ericas (Ericaceae).

It is human to want to explore, to discover new things, then to describe and name them, and finally to relate them to others in our bank of knowledge – a pursuit known in the natural sciences as systematics. Over the past few centuries a huge number of organisms have been studied and embodied in the formal classification of living things. The terminology of this system can appear daunting to the layman but is, in reality, quite simple. The main rankings within the classification system are family (the protea family, Proteaceae, for example), genus (*Leucadendron, Mimetes, Spatalla* and so on) and species (*Leucadendron salignum,* for instance).

In flowering plants, a **family** unites all those which share unique structures, most often floral structures. The implication, in evolutionary terms, is that all members of the family, living and extinct, are descended from the first plant on earth that had this form. Within a family are **genera**, which group together species that share this characteristic as well as other more specialized unifying features pointing to an even closer evolutionary origin. Sometimes, genera are grouped in subfamilies (as they are in the Proteaceae). Species consist of populations of plants which have essentially the same form (the result of the same genetic make-up) and can interbreed freely.

The scientific, or formal, name for a species has two parts, always written in italics, and called a binomial – *Spatalla argentea*, for example. The first part is the genus (*Spatalla*) to which the species belongs and the second, the species identifier within the genus. The combination is unique and universally recognised – '*Spatalla argentea*' is used to describe the same plant in Mandarin, Russian, Spanish, Swahili and any other language. Common names of plants – 'king protea' for instance – appear at first to be more comfortable to use than the formal names but they have shortcomings: in many cases they are not unique, nor universally recognized and, for most of the southern African Proteaceae, there is no common name in general current usage. In this book, the formal name is always used, a common name only where appropriate.

Half-title page: A male orangebreasted sunbird *Nectarinia violacea* on the silver mimetes *Mimetes argenteus*

Page 2: *Leucospermum bolusii* above Kogel Bay in the southwestern Cape

Opposite: *Leucadendron comosum* ssp. *comosum* (male)

Flowering plants first appeared on earth about 125 million years ago. They evolved from some of the cone-bearing species (gymnosperms) which dominated the world's vegetation in the preceding epochs. Fossil remains show that primitive representatives of the Proteaceae were here very soon after this time.

In evolutionary terms, the Proteaceae has always been regarded as very distinct from other flowering plant families, and, moreover, it has been so for a very long time. This conclusion is based largely on the structure of the flowers themselves. Indeed recent research into the genetic make-up of members of the family suggests that, like the Platanaceae (plane trees), the Sabiaceae and Nelumbonaceae (the sacred lotus), all of which evolved early on, it is close to the base of the flowering plants' evolutionary tree.

To see living Proteaceae that most closely resemble some of the ancestral forms, you would have to travel to the northern Queensland region of Australia, where you will find 30-m tall rainforest trees such as *Carnarvonia*

*araliifolia* and *Placospermum coriaceum*, or to the montane heathlands of Tasmania where *Bellendena montana* grows. *Bellendena* is a shrub which produces flowers that have a symmetry different from those of other Proteaceae, so it is believed to represent one of the ancient proteaceous lineages. The flowers of all these primitive forms are borne in loose branched flowerheads quite unlike the highly evolved, densely packed flowerheads of the species in the Cape fynbos and the heathlands of Australia.

If you take a flowerhead of any member of the protea family and look at an individual flower, you will see that the floral sheath (perianth) that covers the style is split into four equal parts which, when the flower is ready to be fertilized, peel back to reveal the pollen presenter as a swollen knob at the end of the style. The individual flowers of *Leucospermum calligerum* are typical. This arrangement is the flower's most immediately obvious distinguishing feature, though there are others – four anthers, for example, and a single-chambered ovary where, after fertilization, one or more seeds grow.

*Leucospermum calligerum*

*Carnarvonia araliifolia* (subfamily Carnarvonioideae)

*Bellendena montana* (subfamily Bellendenoideae)

*Placospermum coriaceum* (subfamily Persoonioideae)

7

Today, the Proteaceae comprises an estimated 1 700 species, most of which are found in the southern hemisphere. The richest areas, in terms of species concentration, are eastern and western Australia and the western Cape region of South Africa. Tropical Africa, tropical South America, Chile and Central America are regions of lesser diversity, while a few species occur in New Guinea, New Caledonia, Borneo, the Malaysian Peninsula, southern India and Southeast Asia. One species occurs as far north as southern Japan.

Australia is the region which has the greatest range of Proteaceae. Not only does this continent boast the greatest number of species, but among these are representatives of all the protea family's seven subfamilies. Africa, the second most species-rich region, has members of only two of the subfamilies. The family's predominantly southern hemisphere distribution pattern is typical of other organisms whose progenitors were once spread over the ancient southern supercontinent of Gondwana.

Some 140 million years ago, Gondwana started to break up into separate land-masses which, eventually, became India, Madagascar and the southern continents we know today. The ancient members of the Proteaceae followed separate evolutionary courses on these now isolated land-masses as they moved to their current positions on the Earth's surface and experienced different geological and climate changes. In places the development of too harsh an environment led to the extinction of some lineages; in others, conditions were favourable for an explosion of different forms. Fossil remains indicate that Antarctica was once home to a variety of proteaceous plants. In New Zealand there are now just two living indigenous members of the family, yet the fossil record clearly shows the land once supported a rich, diverse range of Proteaceae.

The western Australian *Banksia hookeriana* (subfamily Grevilleoideae)

The Madagascan *Faurea forficuliflora* (subfamily Proteoideae)

The Chilean firebush *Embothrium coccineum* (subfamily Grevilleoideae)

The Australian waratah *Telopea speciocissima* (subfamily Grevilleoideae)

The Australian firewheel tree *Stenocarpus sinuatus*
(subfamily Grevilleoideae)

# THE PROTEACEAE IN AFRICA

Africa is home to approximately 400 species of the Proteaceae. These are currently classified into 14 genera: *Protea* (the well-known proteas), *Leucospermum* (the pincushions), *Leucadendron* (leucadendrons), *Serruria* (serrurias), *Vexatorella*, *Aulax*, *Mimetes*, *Orothamnus*, *Spatalla*, *Sorocephalus*, *Paranomus*, *Diastella*, *Faurea*, and *Brabejum*.

Interestingly, *Brabejum* (found only in the western Cape) and the poorly known and increasingly rare Madagascan endemic genus *Malagasia*, each have only one species and belong to the subfamily Grevilleoideae, which has a large number of genera and species in Australasia. All the other African (and Madagascan) genera in the Proteaceae belong to the subfamily Proteoideae.

*Protea*, with some 112 species, is the largest African genus. It also has the greatest area of distribution, ranging from the Cape northwards through Central Africa to East and West Africa. *Faurea* is the only genus common to both Madagascar and mainland Africa;

species occur in temperate evergreen forest, rainforest and deciduous savannah woodland from Knysna in the southern Cape northwards to Ethiopia and westwards to Nigeria and Togo. All the remaining genera, with the exception of a few species of *Leucospermum*, *Leucadendron* and *Vexatorella*, are found in the Cape Floral Region. *Leucospermum* extends up the east coast and eastern highlands of South Africa to the Chimanimani mountains of Zimbabwe, and also up the west coast into Namaqualand. Two species of *Leucadendron* are found along South Africa's east coast. The natural distributions of the remaining genera are restricted to the western and southern Cape, with the exception of one species of *Vexatorella*, which is found on the high slopes of the Kamiesberg mountains of Namaqualand.

The illustrations on the following three pages show representative species of all the southern African genera of the protea family.

## THE PROTEACEAE IN SOUTHERN AFRICA AND THE CAPE

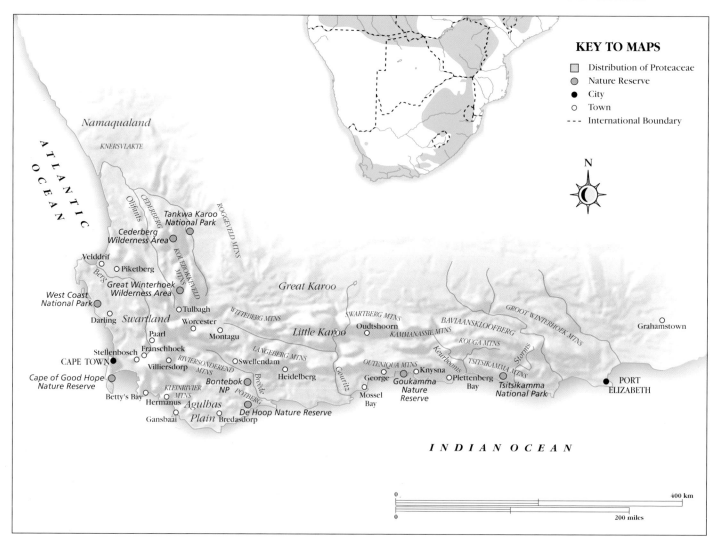

10

*Faurea rochetiana*

*Paranomus dispersus*

*Serruria balanocephala*

*Sorocephalus imbricatus*

The marsh rose *Orothamnus zeyheri*

*Protea pendula*

*Aulax umbellata* (male and female)

*Leucospermum grandiflorum*

*Leucadendron rubrum* (female)

*Vexatorella alpina*

*Mimetes capitulatus*

The wild almond *Brabejum stellatifolium*

*Diastella buekii*

*Spatalla racemosa*

13

# THE PROTEACEAE IN THE CAPE FLORA

*Leucadendron microcephalum* in snow on the southwestern Cape mountains

The great majority of southern African Proteaceae are found in the southwestern and southern Cape. Here the plants are an important component of the Cape flora, which is very different from the floras of other parts of Africa and the world.

Why is there such a variety of flowering plants in this southwestern extremity of the continent? Why is the Proteaceae so richly represented here?

About five million years ago, the climate in this corner of Africa changed, becoming much drier, with the rainfall confined to the coldest season. These changes acted as an evolutionary spur, as the existing plants had to adapt to the new conditions. The broken landscape of the Cape mountains provided a multitude of different habitats which the plants could occupy during the process of adaptation, and a great number of new forms evolved as separate species.

More recently, speciation has also taken place in relatively uniform habitats such as the sandy southern Cape coastal flats – areas of geologically recent deposits.

Here, for example, populations of a large-flowered pincushion in the Albertinia Plateau have become geographically and reproductively isolated from smaller populations found in the southern foothills of the Potberg, near the Breede River mouth. With the passage of time these populations have diverged into two similar but nonetheless distinct species, *Leucospermum praecox* (Albertinia) and *Leucospermum fulgens* (Potberg).

*Protea aspera* and *P. acuminata* are two species with strange geographical distributions. *Protea aspera* is found on the Agulhas Plain, but there is a small and quite isolated population in a valley on the northern side of the Langeberg mountains. *Protea acuminata* is found mostly in the Cederberg mountains, but it too has a far-removed population in the mountains near Villiersdorp, well to the south. Because the isolated groups of these two species cannot freely interbreed with their main populations, they may, over a long time and under the influence of a changing environment, evolve into different forms which will come to be recognized as separate species.

*Leucospermum praecox*

*Protea aspera*

*Protea acuminata*

*Leucospermum fulgens*

The wild almond *Brabejum stellatifolium* next to a mountain pool

Many southern African Proteaceae grow naturally over very restricted ranges, and this is particularly true of the Cape species. Plants which are naturally limited to a specific area are called endemics. Some may be ancient relicts, plants which have survived from bygone ages (palaeoendemics), others quite recently evolved (neoendemics). Paleoendemics were once more widespread but have experienced a history of climatic change which has caused their previous ranges to shrink and confined them to very specific habitats, called 'refugia', in which they can just exist.

*Protea glabra* grows in the Olifants River valley, on the Nieuwoudtville escarpment and on Gifberg, rooted in the cracks of exposed sheets of rock. Many of its structural features are those of the unspecialized Central African proteas – short bracts, simple flowers and a persistent rootstock. The species is almost certainly a survivor of an ancient form that flourished when the western Cape enjoyed a moister, more temperate climate. A similar relict, *Protea rupicola*, occurs only on some of the highest peaks of the western and southern Cape inland ranges. *Sorocephalus alopecurus*, found in moist, sheltered ravines on the Riviersonderend mountains, also has unspecialized features, among them the highly branched arrangement of its flowers that is unlike that of more evolved *Sorocephalus* species.

*Brabejum stellatifolium* is the only surviving African member of the subfamily Grevilleoideae which, as fossil pollen dating from over 100 million years ago shows, was once better represented on this continent.

*Protea rupicola*

*Protea glabra*

*Sorocephalus alopecurus*

# RECENTLY EVOLVED AND LOCALIZED SPECIES

Recently evolved species with very limited ranges – limited probably because they have not had time to spread – are called neoendemics.

Over the past 1.8 million years or so, there have been dramatic fluctuations in the sea level along the southern and western Cape coastlines, periodically exposing areas of sand and rock that had previously been under water. These sites were colonized by plants derived from existing species but changed through having to adapt to the newly available habitats to become species in their own right. The outwardly simple flowerheads of *Spatalla ericoides*, a plant endemic to a few square kilometres of the Agulhas coastal plain, are actually complex structures, and the plant probably evolved from a less specialized *Spatalla* species from the nearby coastal mountains. In all likelihood *Leucospermum tomentosum*, from the sand plain of the Cape's west coast, is also a recently evolved species; it too has a number of specialized flower and leaf features.

The curious but seldom seen *Protea inopina* occupies a very limited habitat in the Citrusdal mountains, and appears to have evolved in recent times as a stabilized mutant from its close relative, the common and widespread waboom *Protea nitida*, which it closely resembles. Not far from here – on one peak in the Kouebokkeveld mountains – there is a single group of about 50 individual plants of the extraordinary and very beautiful *Leucadendron bonum*, an example of an extreme endemic.

*Leucospermum tomentosum*

*Protea inopina*

*Spatalla ericoides*

*Leucadendron bonum*

# CLOSELY RELATED SPECIES

When distinct but closely related species are separated geographically, they are described as vicariants. Vicariants are descended from a common ancestral species. In the mountainous western and southern Cape, for example, the high peaks and deep valleys became 'islands' providing geographical and reproductive isolation for plant populations that were once widespread but were later fragmented due to climatic change.

The blushing bride *Serruria florida*, a rarity restricted to a few hectares in the Assegaibos valley at the head of the Berg River near Franschhoek in the Western Cape province, is characterized by its large white bracts, which become flushed pink at maturity. *Serruria rosea*, its vicariant, grows on the opposite side of the Berg River, in the Wemmershoek valley and adjacent areas. Although this species has smaller, permanently red-flushed bracts, the relationship between the two is quite apparent.

*Leucospermum cordifolium* is common on the Agulhas Plain, thriving on acidic soils derived from Table Mountain sandstone. Its vicariant, *Leucospermum patersonii*, is restricted to the limestone hills, with their alkaline soils, of the geologically recent Bredasdorp formation close to the sandstone. Here, vicarious species have evolved as a result of the adaptation, by a previously existing species, to two sharply contrasting but adjacent habitats.

*Leucospermum cordifolium*

The blushing bride *Serruria florida*

*Leucospermum patersonii*

*Serruria rosea*

The king protea *Protea cynaroides* on the Cape Peninsula

The eastern Cape dwarf form of the king protea

*Protea cynaroides* on the Riviersonderend mountains

One of the Hottentots Holland mountains forms of *Protea cynaroides*

The individuals of some plant species differ very little from each other, while in others there may be so much variation that it is difficult to define them. Large differences between populations of a single species over its distribution range are often an indication that they are on the way to becoming distinct species in their own right. *Protea cynaroides*, for example, is one that has evolved local races whose differences are perceptible, but insufficient at present for them each to be recognized as separate species.

The king protea *Protea cynaroides* (South Africa's national flower) is found from the Cederberg to the Cape Peninsula and eastwards to Grahamstown, occupying a variety of habitats from sea level up to 1 500 metres. Its leaves may be round, oval or narrowly elliptic; the flowerheads may be small (120 mm in diameter in the Port Elizabeth area) or huge (up to 300 mm in diameter in the Langeberg and Outeniqua mountains). The bracts are usually covered with dense, silky hairs but can in some areas be quite hairless. Bract colour ranges from pink through crimson to yellow and creamy-white. Each geographical race of *P. cynaroides* has its own genetically controlled flowering season. Commercial growers are able to produce blooms for the cut-flower trade throughout the year by cultivating a selection of the spring, summer, autumn and winter flowering races.

Successful species are usually adaptable, efficient reproducers, and well able to compete with others, at least under prevailing environmental conditions. The Cape has its fair share of successful Proteaceae. It also has some that are naturally rare, inefficient at reproducing themselves and apparently struggling to compete with other plants. These appear unable to spread from their limited range.

*Mimetes cucullatus*, the most widespread species in its genus, is a very successful species. Usually large, vigorous populations are found from the Kouebokkeveld mountains southwards to the southwestern Cape mountains and the Agulhas Plain (where it is common) and then eastwards through the Outeniqua and Swartberg mountains to the Kouga mountains. In contrast, *Mimetes hottentoticus* is confined to the summit of Kogelberg and an adjacent peak in the Western Cape, apparently unable to break out of its narrow habitat – permanently damp, acidic, peaty, south-facing mountain slopes which receive a lot of moisture in summer from cloud.

*Protea punctata*, widespread and common on the drier inland mountains of the western and southern Cape, is also successful, growing and reproducing vigorously to form dense stands of large shrubs on very dry sites. The exceedingly rare *Protea holosericea*, on the other hand, has never managed to spread beyond its high, arid, rocky habitat on Sawedge Peak and the neighbouring Rabiesberg east of the town of Worcester.

*Leucadendron salignum* is almost ubiquitous in the fynbos biome: no other leucadendron can tolerate such a wide range of habitats. A persistent rootstock allows it to resprout after fire, further enhancing its competitiveness.

*Mimetes hottentoticus*

*Mimetes cucullatus*

*Leucadendron salignum* near the Cape of Good Hope

*Protea holosericea*

*Protea punctata*

# EXTINCTIONS

Two western Cape Proteaceae – *Mimetes stokoei* and *Leucadendron spirale* – are known to have become extinct during the past century. The latter has not been seen since 1933.

*Mimetes stokoei* was discovered, in 1922 by T.P. Stokoe, on a small plateau in the Kogelberg reserve near Kleinmond. The species then consisted of a single group of less than a dozen plants, most of which died over the following 20 years. A fire then swept the area and, after the burn, about ten plants grew from seed dropped by the previous group. These also died away over the years, and by 1950 none remained. In 1965 another fire burnt the area but only one seedling appeared, only to die, in 1969, without flowering. No more plants of this species have ever been found. *M. stokoei* most probably became extinct quite naturally, a process which is just as much a part of evolution as the appearance of new life forms.

Uncaring landowners and the spread of invasive, alien *Acacia* species have pushed the smallest of all proteas to the brink of extinction in its natural habitat. Two substantial populations of *Protea odorata* once grew in renosterveld north of Cape Town; today, just a few individuals survive – under huge threat – on a private farm. However, the introduction of some cultivated plants to the Riverlands Nature Reserve, where the species used to grow, may stave off its extinction in the wild.

*Mimetes stokoei*, now extinct

*Protea odorata*

*Leucadendron concavum* (male)

*Serruria cyanoides*

*Leucadendron singulare* in the Kammanassie mountains

Rare plants hold a special fascination for us, but rarity is often difficult to define. Conservationists consider a species to be rare when the total number of plants growing naturally in the wild is small but the populations are neither endangered nor vulnerable. In South Africa, 74 Proteaceae are classified as vulnerable or endangered, and a great many more are rare.
A surprising number of naturally rare species exist as very small populations in conserved areas. Unfortunately, though, there are many more that are rare because their numbers have been greatly reduced by the effects of growing human populations.

*Leucadendron singulare*, from the Kammanassie mountains, is naturally rare: fewer than 300 plants of this beautiful, silver, dwarf species grow among the rocks of the remote summit of Mannetjiesberg. *Leucadendron concavum* is also a naturally rare species, restricted to a very small site in the Cederberg Wilderness Area.

The Cape Peninsula endemic *Serruria cyanoides* tells a different story. This plant was once common on the Cape Flats, but it has been completely obliterated there, over the last several decades, by urban sprawl and now survives only above the seaside town of Fish Hoek and on Hout Bay's Karbonkelberg.

Although the reasons are sometimes obscure, natural rarity is a feature of a lot of the species in many families of the Cape flora. There is scarcely a square kilometre in the western and southern Cape that does not support several rarities. The majority of these rarities have just a few small populations, sometimes only one. The region's huge floral diversity and the high percentage of rare plants pose almost insurmountable problems for conservation authorities who are anxious to protect as much of this treasure as limited resources allow against ever increasing demands from a burgeoning human population. The Proteaceae illustrated here are all naturally rare, growing in pristine conserved areas.

*Mimetes arboreus*, a potentially long-lived, tree-like species growing up to 6 m in height, is confined to the Kogelberg reserve to the east of Cape Town. It is usually solitary but sometimes occurs in small groups. The thick bark of mature specimens provides some protection from fire, but the very few seedlings that are produced by this species are destroyed if they are burnt so that too-frequent fires allow only a handful of these plants to survive and reproduce.

The Cape of Good Hope reserve is the sole habitat of the tiny, trailing *Serruria decumbens*, which can be seen on the hills around Olifantsbos. The high peaks above Wemmershoek and Villiersdorp are home to *Sorocephalus teretifolius*, while *Leucadendron cadens* can only be seen along the summit ridges of the Witteberg, near Matjiesfontein on the fringes of the Great Karoo. *Leucospermum winteri* was discovered in the Langeberg in 1974. It used only to be known from scattered populations on the higher peaks between Garcia's Pass and Cloete's Pass but, very recently, a larger group has been found on the south side of these mountains.

*Mimetes arboreus*

*Leucospermum winteri*

*Serruria decumbens*

*Sorocephalus teretifolius*

*Leucadendron cadens* (male)

29

*Leucadendron macowanii* (male)

*Leucospermum arenarium*

*Leucadendron floridum* (male)

When the habitats of naturally rare species are impacted by residential development or expanding agricultural activities the inevitable consequence is a catastrophic decline in their numbers.

*Leucadendron macowanii*, a Cape Peninsula endemic, was described from plants growing at Wynberg in 1888. These have long since disappeared. Today, the only surviving population of the species occurs at Smitswinkel Bay and a little farther south in the neighbouring area of the Cape of Good Hope reserve.

The destruction of *Leucadendron floridum* has been even more dramatic. In 1900 populations of this wetlands species thrived at Kuils River and in the Cape metropolitan areas of Bellville, Rondebosch and Wynberg, but

they were fast crowded out by advancing suburbia. The species could still be found growing at several sites on Bergvliet farm as late as 1918, but these too are now gone. Today, a few outliers struggle to survive around Ocean View near Kommetjie but, fortunately, several populations also grow within the boundaries of the Cape of Good Hope reserve, its final refuge.

A few years ago the very localized *Leucospermum arenarium* looked fairly secure in its sandy habitat between the small Cape West Coast towns of Aurora and Redelinghuis. Now, most of the plants have been ploughed up as agriculture expands relentlessly into the west coast sandveld with the cultivation of cereals and seed potatoes.

Male and female plants of *Aulax umbellata*

The wild almond *Brabejum stellatifolium* is the only species in its genus. It is also the only continental African representative of the Grevilleoideae, a subfamily of the Proteaceae to which many species elsewhere in the world belong. As such, it is only distantly related to the other African Proteaceae.

*Brabejum* can mature into an 8-m tree. Old specimens, such as those planted by Van Riebeeck three-and-a-half centuries ago at Kirstenbosch near Cape Town, are massive. This species grows in damp situations, either in forest or alongside streams. Despite its potential longevity, it is adapted to fire as it can resprout after a burn – which is probably why, alone among members of a subfamily that once flourished in the region, it has survived.

*Aulax* is the third smallest of the African genera of the protea family: it contains just three species, all found in the fynbos of the southwestern and southern Cape. Male and female flowerheads are carried on separate plants, a feature shared by only one other African genus, *Leucadendron*. The male flowerheads comprise soft, yellow spikes; female plants produce cones which become woody with age. In two of the species, *A. umbellata* and *A. cancellata*, the cones retain the seeds until they are burnt by one of the fires that are a recurrent feature of their fynbos habitat. The seeds are then released and drop onto the soil to germinate in an environment cleared of vegetation. *A. pallasia* can grow from seed but plants can also resprout after a burn.

*Aulax pallasia* (male)

*Aulax cancellata* (female)

*Brabejum stellatifolium*, the wild almond

# THE GENUS *PROTEA*

Carl Linnaeus, the renowned 18th-century Swedish botanist, is regarded as the father of systematics, the universally accepted system of the classification of life forms. Just why he gave (in 1735) the name Protea to a handful of the relatively few plants then known from the Cape remains unclear. Proteus was the god of Ancient Greek mythology who could change his form at will. Linnaeus claimed that he gave the name because of the plants' great variability but, in fact, he had never seen living examples or even dried material of them and described them only from etchings of the 24 different forms known at that time.

These plants had been collected around the Dutch East India Company's settlement at the Cape and later illustrated in Europe. Linnaeus could never have realised how apt his name was, for, in the ensuing centuries, as botanical exploration of the Cape's flora extended ever further afield, the extraordinary diversity of the proteas became evident.

Because *Protea* was the first genus of the family to have been formally described, Proteaceae was taken as the family name. In this case, the classical allusion is even more apt as some of the genera are so different in appearance that it is difficult for laymen to see the relationship.

*Protea caespitosa*

*Protea scolopendriifolia*

*Protea repens*, the sugarbush

*Protea lacticolor*

*Protea effusa*

*Protea cynaroides*, the king protea

35

*Protea lorea*

*Protea laevis*

*Protea mucronifolia*

*Protea lepidocarpodendron*

*Protea* is the most widespread genus of the southern Africa Proteaceae. Unlike all the other genera, substantial numbers of *Protea* species are found both in the Cape Floral Region, an area of predominantly winter or all-year round rainfall (70 species), and in the subtropical and tropical parts of southern Africa which receive their rain mainly in summer (19 species).

In all of the vegetation types in which proteas are found – the fynbos of the Cape and high mountain peaks further north, the grasslands and savannah of the summer rainfall regions – fire is a regular event. Proteas have evolved several strategies to cope with burns. Many of the dwarf and low-growing species can resprout from underground stems (like *Protea scolopendriifolia* and *P. lorea*) or rootstocks (for example, *P. tenax*, *P. enervis*, *P. welwitschii* ssp.*hirta* and *P. asymmetrica*) after fire has burnt off their above-ground parts. Some of the large growing proteas (among them *P. caffra* and *P. nitida*) have thick, corky bark which protects the living tissue beneath it from fire damage.

Many of the Cape species, including *P. repens* and *P. lepidocarpodendron*, have evolved flowerheads which become woody after flowering. These retain their seeds until the heat of a fire opens them and the seed falls, onto ground cleared of cover, to germinate after the first substantial rainfall. This strategy is known as 'serotiny'.

*Protea* species differ markedly not only in size and habit but also in the shape of the leaves and the flowerheads. The common, unifying feature of the genus, however, is the form of the flowerhead. In proteas the individual flowers are packed into a receptacle surrounded by a series of coloured bracts. The upper bracts cover the mass of flowers to a greater or lesser extent. In many Cape flora species the bracts completely surround the flowers, as they do in *Protea compacta*. The beauty of proteas derives mainly from the colouring and texture of the bracts.

In most species, the flowerheads arise at the ends of stems, but there are some specialized proteas, such as *Protea subulifolia*, whose heads are arranged along the branches or clustered at the base of the plant. Leaf size and shape vary enormously from species to species but all (except when young) are hard and stiff. A few species like *Protea pityphylla* have needle-like leaves. If left undisturbed, some proteas – the waboom *Protea nitida*, for example – can grow to the size of small trees. Others are dwarf. Among the most fascinating of the smallest forms are some fynbos species which grow from underground stems as tufts of leaves which are virtually indistinguishable from the surrounding restios (Cape reeds, in the family Restionaceae) until the plants produce their flowerheads, often at ground level. *Protea lorea* is one of the most striking examples.

*Protea pityphylla*

*Protea compacta*

*Protea subulifolia*

The waboom *Protea nitida*

*Protea rubropilosa*

*Protea asymmetrica*

*Protea welwitschii*

*Protea caffra* ssp. *caffra*

*Protea tenax*

*Protea enervis*

This genus has not been comprehensively studied and reviewed so the way in which the species are currently recognized may change.

This genus is unique among the African genera of the Proteaceae in that it is essentially tropical and subtropical. Only one species, *Faurea macnaughtonii*, is found in the Cape Floral Region. This large tree is rare and only found growing in isolated groups in forests in the southern Cape and eastern South Africa. Its presence in the Knysna forests has nothing to do with the evolution of the fynbos in the Cape. On the contrary, the patches of forest in the southern Cape are relictual, the remains of ancient forests which covered most of southern Africa when the climate here was once wetter and more uniform. *Faurea macnaughtonii* is one of the relatively few tree types which have managed to

hang on here as the environment became drier and the forests shrunk, losing many of the species that are still found in similar forests farther north.

Of the 14 African species of *Faurea*, six occur in the subcontinent. Of these, three are endemic to the region – *F. macnaughtonii*, *F. galpinii* from the fringes of montane forests in Swaziland and Mpumalanga, and *F. rubriflora* from a similar habitat in eastern Zimbabwe. The other three species which are found in southern Africa, *F. rochetiana*, *F. saligna* and *F. delevoyi*, have a much wider African distribution.

In *Faurea*, the flowers are arranged along a spike. These flowerheads are considered to be unspecialized so that *Faurea* is probably an old genus representing some of the Proteaceae present in Africa long before some of the Cape genera had evolved.

*Faurea galpinii*

*Faurea macnaughtonii* in forest on the KwaZulu-Natal coast

*Faurea rubriflora*

*Faurea saligna*

43

*Leucadendron* contains 83 species and is the second largest genus of the family in Africa. Unlike *Protea,* the largest genus, it is however only found in South Africa, with the great majority of its species in the western and southern Cape. Two subspecies of *Leucadendron spissifolium* grow along the Eastern Cape Province and KwaZulu-Natal coast, where there are outcrops of rock similar to the Table Mountain sandstone of the Cape fold mountains. *Leucadendron pondoense,* as its name suggests, is found only in the Pondoland area of the Eastern Cape on the same rock formation. This genus is not closely related to any of the other genera.

Leucadendrons, like the plants of genus *Aulax,* are dioecious (that is, male and female flowers are produced on different plants) but this characteristic has apparently evolved quite independently in these two genera. Not only are leucadendrons dioecious but in some instances (*Leucadendron rubrum* for example), male and female flowerheads are so different in appearance that it is hard to believe they are of the same species. In others, like *Leucadendron sorocephalodes,* male and female are very similar. This separation of the sexes enforces cross-pollination. In most cases, 'cross-' pollination is effected by insects, but in a few others, by wind. In a wild population of leucadendrons, the males always open first and fade last, while the female plants flower for a short period at the peak of the male flowering flush – an elegant strategy to ensure availability of fresh pollen to fertilize the females.

*Leucadendron laxum* (female)

*Leucadendron levisanus* (male)

The silver tree *Leucadendron argenteum* (male)

*Leucadendron lanigerum* ssp. *lanigerum* (female)

*Leucadendron loeriense* (female)

45

*Leucadendron olens* (male)

The Cape Proteaceae have evolved many strategies in the competition with other plants to attract pollinators to ensure the next generation. In *Protea*, the bracts surrounding the flowerhead are enlarged and brightly coloured, enclosing the styles. Quite the opposite happens in *Leucospermum*, whose bracts are tiny, green and insignificant while the styles are enlarged and brightly coloured. *Leucadendron* uses yet another technique: both the bracts and the styles are small and insignificant but, in most species, the normally green leaves around the base of each flowerhead become enlarged and flushed brilliant yellow during the flowering period. This process can transform the landscape. Unlike some other Proteaceae, leucadendrons seldom grow as isolated individuals: they are most often seen in large, dense stands. In winter and spring (their prime flowering times) the fynbos veld is lit up by glowing patches of yellow and gold leucadendrons in full bloom. Yellow is a colour readily visible and attractive to insects such as bees, flies and beetles, which carry out the crucial job of cross-pollination in the great majority of species. A few leucadendrons like *L. glaberrimum* ssp. *erubescens* as well as the Langkloof and Kouebokkeveld forms of *L. salignum* take on rich crimson tones at certain times of the year. The latter species has been used to breed a number of crimson-coloured hybrids like *Leucadendron* 'safari sunset' which are cultivated commercially for the cut-flower trade.

*Leucadendron nitidum* (male)

*Leucadendron arcuatum* (male)

*Leucadendron nervosum* (female)

Unlike the seeds of different species of *Protea* and *Leucospermum*, which all look more or less the same within each genus, leucadendron seeds vary enormously. Some are flat and winged, others are nuts of various shapes and can be either smooth or hairy. The seeds are carried in cones which are a distinctive feature of female leucadendron plants that makes them immediately recognizable in the veld. In all of the species with flat seeds and in a few with nut-like seeds, the seeds are retained in the cones which, with age, grow woody and hard. There they can stay for years, safe from rodents and insects, ready to germinate after a fire opens the cones to release them (a strategy called 'serotiny'). This protection is carried to the extreme in *Leucadendron platyspermum*, in whose massive cones the seeds actually germinate before being released. The cones of the majority of the *Leucadendron* species which have nut-type seeds are not serotinous but shed their seeds a few months after flowering. Rodents collect the seeds and hoard them in their underground burrows where any that are not eaten lie until the passing of a fire stimulates them to germinate.

Much has been made of the story of the *Leucadendon* species whose nut-like seeds retain the dried out, opened floral sheath (perianth) as a parachute to allow the seed to drift in the wind some way from the parent plant. This works somewhat with the seed of *Leucadendron rubrum* but, in all honesty, the big seeds of the silver tree (*L. argenteum*) fly pretty much like stones and it would take a gale to move them far from their parent plant.

*Leucadendron nobile* (female)

*Leucadendron sorocephalodes* (male)

*Leucadendron discolor* (male)

*Leucadendron microcephalum* (female)

*Leucadendron tinctum* (male)

*Leucadendron elimense* ssp. *vyeboomense* (male)

49

# THE GENERA *VEXATORELLA* AND *DIASTELLA*

The discovery of the species now known as *Vexatorella latebrosa* (see page 123) posed a problem. The plant was certainly a member of the protea family, but it was different from anything known at the time – so different that it could not be placed in any of the existing genera. In 1984 a new genus, *Vexatorella* (which translates as 'the little trouble-maker'), was created to accommodate the new plant. Two other species, which were previously placed, for want of a better home, in *Leucospermum*, were then moved to the new genus.

Unlike most of the species in the other Cape genera, *Vexatorella* species are not found in the mountains of the southwestern Cape. All species in this genus grow in dry fynbos on the fringe of arid Succulent Karoo vegetation. Their flowerheads are very like those of the pincushions in appearance but share features with leucadendrons –

the floral bracts become enlarged and woody after the flower is fertilized.

*Diastella*, a small genus of seven species, is one of a group of four closely related genera which also includes *Leucospermum*, *Mimetes* and *Orothamnus*. It is confined to the heart of the southwestern Cape's fynbos. *Diastella divaricata* ssp. *divaricata* is a common shrublet on the Cape Peninsula mountains, and all the other members of the genus grow within a 200-km radius of here. Their most obvious distinguishing feature is the very small, soft, hairy flowerheads whose bracts never become woody. The only known natural *Diastella* hybrid is not, as one would suppose, a cross between two species in the genus, but between *D. thymelaeoides* and a pincushion, *Leucospermum oleifolium*. This hybrid confirms the close relationship between *Diastella* and *Leucospermum*.

*Diastella divaricata* ssp. *divaricata*

*Vexatorella obtusata* ssp. *albomontana*

*Diastella thymelaeoides* ssp. *meridiana*          *Diastella fraterna*          *Vexatorella latebrosa*

*Mimetes hirtus*

*Mimetes argenteus*

These two genera are confined to the Cape Floral Region. In *Mimetes*, clusters of a few flowers grow straight off the flowering stem next to the uppermost leaves. This arrangement, although it is not immediately apparent, is much like that in *Leucospermum* but in this genus the flowerheads are on stalks. *Orothamnus* has only one species, *O. zeyheri*, the celebrated marsh rose, whose hanging flowerheads – dominated by large pink or crimson bracts – are produced one at a time at the end of the continually growing flowering stem. The three genera are closely related.

Some of the *Mimetes* species are among the loveliest of the Cape flora's flowering plants. The four silver mimetes – *Mimetes argenteus*, *M. arboreus*, *M. splendidus* and *M. hottentoticus* – are exceptional in their beauty (the fifth member of this group, *M. stokoei*, is extinct). Their attraction derives not only from their shimmering foliage. In the first three, the flowers are not especially colourful but, during flowering, the leaves surrounding them take on delicate shades of pink or apricot that enhance their silver sheen; in *M. hottentoticus*, the flowers themselves are colourful. *M. hirtus* and *M. capitulatus* are also striking plants. *Mimetes pauciflorus*, from the southern Cape mountains, is unique within the genus: the bracts that clasp its flower clusters are long and bright yellow, an advanced adaptation for bird pollination.

*Orothamnus zeyheri,* the marsh rose

*Mimetes splendidus*

53

# THE GENUS *LEUCOSPERMUM*

Pincushions, as the species of *Leucospermum* are popularly known, are probably as familiar as the proteas: some are well-known garden plants, several are commercially important. Some of the larger-flowered species are strikingly ornamental, especially *L. cordifolium*, *L. lineare* and *L. tottum*. These have been selected and hybridized to produce cultivars which are cultivated commercially in South Africa, Israel, Australia, New Zealand, California and Hawaii.

The most obvious distinguishing features of the genus are the very prominent, stout, colourful styles, the small inconspicuous bracts surrounding the flowerheads – quite unlike those of the proteas – and the teeth at the end of each leaf. Individual species vary, ranging from trees with stout trunks (such as *L. conocarpodendron*) to plants growing flat on the ground (like *L. prostratum*).

The colourful large-flowered species (*L. pluridens* for example) are visited for their nectar by the Cape sugar-bird *Promerops caffer* and by sunbirds, especially the orangebreasted sunbird *Nectarinia violacea*. Tiny ground-hugging species with dull-coloured flowerheads like *L. hamatum* are believed to be pollinated by small rodents, though this has not yet been conclusively proved. The same rodents like to feed on the pale, nut-like seeds which are released from the heads as they age. Ants, attracted by a fleshy appendage on the seeds, collect them and remove them underground, where they are safe from predation and can germinate after a fire.

*Leucospermum pluridens*

*Leucospermum formosum*

*Leucospermum truncatulum*

*Leucospermum lineare*

*Leucospermum profugum*

*Leucospermum cuneiforme*

There are 48 species of *Leucospermum*, most of which are confined to the Cape Floral Region. *Leucospermum cuneiforme*, however, extends a short way up the eastern Cape coast, while two species (*Leucospermum gerrardii* and *L. innovans*) occur in KwaZulu-Natal and a single species (*L. saxosum*) in Mpumalanga and Zimbabwe. Two species (*Leucospermum rodolentum* and *L. praemorsum*) are also found well into Namaqualand.

The greatest concentration of *Leucospermum* species is on the Agulhas Plain where 30 per cent of all species are found. Most of these have recently evolved on this geologically young land surface. It is away from here, in the eastern and northern parts of the distribution of the genus, that species with unspecialized or primitive features like *L. saxosum*, *L. innovans*, *L. gerrardii* and *L. cuneiforme* grow. In these, the flowerhead is little more than a contracted version of the spike-like form which

characterizes the flowerhead of *Faurea* species. *Leucospermum saxosum* has a remarkably broken distribution, with populations in the Chimanimani mountains in eastern Zimbabwe that are separated by the Limpopo valley from a few, far-distant relictual groups in the Mpumalanga Drakensberg. The heavy, nut-like seeds of this species are, like others, ant-dispersed and therefore not spread widely, so how does one explain such a curious distribution? The answer probably lies in the geological past: about 65 million years ago there was a continuous land surface, stretching from the Cape to Central Africa, on which ancestral forms of fynbos grew. The mountains which were formed more recently in the east, as the earth's crust shifted and sheared, probably fragmented ancestral populations of species like *L. saxosum*, whose modern descendants only survive as isolated groups on the highest ground.

*Leucospermum oleifolium*

*Leucospermum hypophyllocarpodendron* ssp. *hypophyllocarpodendron*

*Leucospermum hamatum*

# THE GENUS *SERRURIA*

*Serruria villosa*

All the genera of the southern African Proteaceae save two – this genus and *Faurea* – have been studied, and definitive accounts of them, called revisions, written and published. *Serruria* is currently being revised by Dr John Rourke at the National Botanical Institute's Compton Herbarium at Kirstenbosch in the Cape. In consequence, it is not always possible to make categorical statements about the genus, nor have all the species' names been finally fixed.

Revisions involve a great deal of field work in addition to the necessary laboratory studies, and one of the results in *Serruria* has been the recognition of several new species like *Serruria gremialis* as the concepts of previously recognized but poorly known species have

been refined. Other species have been known, albeit poorly, for some while but never formally described and named; *S. effusa* is one of these. Quite independently, a disproportionately large number of brand new *Serruria* species (*S. deluvialis*, for example ) has been discovered in the last few years. One of these new species, *Serruria lacunosa*, was only discovered in the mid-1990s by members of the Protea Atlas Project. This find had special significance because it extended the northern limit of the geographical range of the genus considerably – to the Table Mountain-sandstone massif of the Matsikamma, which stands high over the southeast corner of Namaqualand's arid Knersvlakte. *Serruria rebeloi* (see page 123) is another of the recent finds.

*Serruria effusa*

*Serruria gremialis*

*Serruria kraussii*

*Serruria* is one of the genera of the Proteaceae which are strictly confined to the Cape Floral Region. In fact it is essentially limited to the area of winter rainfall with only one species, *Serruria fasciflora*, extending beyond this, eastwards to the Langeberg mountains near Mossel Bay. This species has the widest distribution in the genus.

Many other species have limited ranges, and most are restricted to specific habitats. *Serruria villosa*, for example, is found only in the southern Cape Peninsula, where it grows in colonies on slopes and flats in white sandy soil derived from Table Mountain sandstone. *Serruria kraussii* is a rare plant, known only from three populations in the Hottentots Hollands mountains, where it prefers granitic soils. *Serruria effusa* occurs in arid fynbos on the western side of the Cederberg range at low altitudes, often in places where the sandstone meets heavier shale soils or on the sandveld of the western coastal plain.

Once much more common on the sand flats north and west of Cape town, *Serruria aemula* is becoming increasingly rare as the city's urban and industrial sprawl spreads inexorably wider.

*Serruria phylicoides*, previously known as *S. barbigera*, is an attractive species, in cultivation as a garden plant, with a relatively large natural range in the Du Toit's Kloof, Hottentots Hollands, Riviersonderend and Klein-rivier mountains. It has a variety of forms varying from a low, dense mat on the summit of Bokkop near Villiers-dorp to a virtually unbranched, erect shrub above Greyton.

*Serruria rubricaulis*

*Serruria deluvialis*

*Serruria aemula*

*Serruria triternata*

*Serruria aitonii*

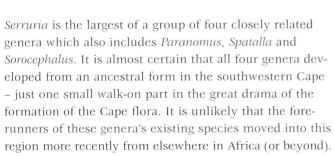

*Serruria phylicoides*

*Serruria flagellifolia*

*Serruria* is the largest of a group of four closely related genera which also includes *Paranomus, Spatalla* and *Sorocephalus*. It is almost certain that all four genera developed from an ancestral form in the southwestern Cape – just one small walk-on part in the great drama of the formation of the Cape flora. It is unlikely that the forerunners of these genera's existing species moved into this region more recently from elsewhere in Africa (or beyond).

As things stand at present, *Serruria* has about 55 species so that it is, in fact, one of the largest of the African genera of the protea family. The final tally will probably differ slightly from this number when the systematic treatment of the genus is finalised.

The unifying and characteristic feature of *Serruria* is the form of the species' leaves, which are divided into segments whose cross-section is circular. One other genus, *Paranomus*, has species with divided leaves but these are different: the segments of *Paranomus* have a groove on top. None of the *Serruria* species grows to any great size; most are small shrubs. But there are some unusual forms. *Serruria flagellifolia*, for example, has a few long, thin, sparse, trailing stems, carrying equally thin, hardly divided, upturned leaves. These creep through the surrounding vegetation so that they are nearly impossible to see. The plants of most of the species are killed outright by fires and the populations regenerate from seed but some species like *S. gremialis* and *S. rubricaulis* can coppice from their underground rootstocks. *Serruria* seeds, like those of *Mimetes* and *Leucospermum* are collected by ants and stored underground.

*Paranomus longicaulis*

*Paranomus dregei*

Like serrurias, *Paranomus* species have divided leaves. A distinctive feature of the genus, however, is that individual plants of some of its species can carry, simultaneously, both normal leaves and ones which are hardly divided or even undivided. *Paranomus longicaulis*, *P. dregei* and *P. adiantifolius* fall into this category. *Paranomus* flowerheads are thick, stiff spikes, along which are arranged clusters of four flowers. The spikes, which become woody with age, are elongated in species such as *P. tomentosus*, but almost round in others, among them *P. capitatus*.

There are only 18 species of *Paranomus*, but the genus has a far wider range than *Serruria*. *Paranomus reflexus* for instance comes from the Elandsberg mountains near Port Elizabeth at the eastern end of the Cape Floral Region.

The Swartberg range, where there are no serrurias, is home to three *Paranomus* species: *P. dregei*, *P. centaureoides* and *P. dispersus*. *P. longicaulis*, *P. roodebergensis* and *P. spathulatus* grow in arid fynbos on the fringes of the Little Karoo, while *P. esterhuyseniae* is endemic to the dry fynbos slopes of the Kouga mountains.

All the *Paranomus* species are shrubs, and some can attain fairly large size: in the Cederberg, for example, *P. tomentosus*, if left unburned for long enough, can grow into a 3-m high tree with a substantial trunk. None of the species, with the possible exception of a form of *P. spathulatus*, which grows on Gamkaberg in the Little Karoo near Oudtshoorn, resprouts after a fire; regeneration is from seed, which is soon lost from the spikes after flowering. *Paranomus* species are not serotinous.

*Paranomus capitatus*

*Paranomus tomentosus*

*Paranomus adiantifolius*

# THE GENERA *SOROCEPHALUS* AND *SPATALLA*

These two very closely related genera are small; *Spatalla* has just twenty species and *Sorocephalus*, eleven. All of the *Sorocephalus* and most of the *Spatalla* species are found in the winter rainfall area of the southwestern Cape; *Spatalla confusa* has a wider range which includes the Swartberg. *Spatalla parilis* grows along the Langeberg. *Spatalla barbigera* has an unusual distribution: the coastal Langeberg and Outeniqua mountains as well as the inland Swartberg range.

All the plants in these two genera are small, sometimes mat-like shrubs. In *Spatalla*, single flowers or clusters of three are arranged along a soft spike at the end of a stem. In *Sorocephalus*, the clusters contain four or more flowers. The flowerhead of *Sorocephalus teretifolius* is unique within the genus in that its flowers are packed into a receptacle rather than arranged in discrete clusters along a spike. Species of *Spatalla* are thought to have evolved from ancestral forms like the species of *Sorocephalus* here today because a reduction in the number of flowers in each cluster in the flowerhead is considered to represent a specialized development.

Sorocephalus lanatus is fairly common and widespread in the Kouebokkeveld and Cederberg, S. clavigerus has a much smaller range in the Hottentots Holland and Kleinrivier mountains. All the other species in the genus are either rare or very rare. There is little doubt that many are palaeoendemics – survivors, in very limited habitats, of a time when the climate all over the southwestern Cape was cooler and wetter. This genus thus represents an opportunity to see evolution in progress. The relictual species may well be on the road to extinction, hastened unnaturally by too-frequent man-made fires in their last mountain refuges. In contrast, many Spatalla species are naturally vigorous, growing in sizeable populations.

*Spatalla prolifera*

*Spatalla parilis*

*Sorocephalus palustris*

*Spatalla incurva*

*Sorocephalus scabridus*

*Leucospermum saxosum* in Zimbabwe's Chimanimani mountains

*Protea caffra* ssp. *gazensis*

*Protea wentzeliana*

*Protea angolensis* var. *divaricata*

In southern Africa, Proteaceae are absent from the humid lowland regions of southern Mozambique as well as the arid areas in the west, north of the Orange River. Only *Protea gaguedi*, which tolerates drier conditions than the other tropical species, extends into Namibia (in the very north) and Botswana (in the northeast). In the east of the subcontinent, this species reaches as far south as northern KwaZulu-Natal. Another very widespread tropical protea, *Protea welwitschii*, reaches even farther south, to the coast near Durban.

*Leucospermum saxosum* is the only pincushion found in the tropics. Its largest population is in the Chimanimani mountains which straddle the Zimbabwe/Mozambique border and is found in the fynbos on the quartzite rocks of this range. Two proteas – *P. enervis* (an endemic) and *P. wentzeliana* – are also part of this vegetation.

Both species are typical of a group of tropical proteas which characteristically grow as small, isolated populations in poor soils on the highest mountains. Two others – *P. dracomontana* and the endemic *P. asymmetrica* – grow on Mount Inyangani, in the Eastern Highlands of Zimbabwe.

The other tropical proteas grow in a very different habitat – the extensive areas of woodland and grasslands at mid and high altitudes. *Protea angolensis*, *P. caffra* ssp. *gazensis* and *P. petiolaris*, all species with wide ranges, are found in these areas, as are *Faurea rochetiana* and *F. saligna*, which are both small trees. The remaining tropical *Faurea* species, namely *F. rubriflora* from the montane forests of eastern Zimbabwe and neighbouring Mozambique, and *F. delevoyi*, typically found in riverine forests at lower altitudes, are large trees.

*Protea gaguedi*

*Protea petiolaris*

# SUBTROPICAL PROTEACEAE IN SOUTH AFRICA

The summer rainfall areas of South Africa, together with Swaziland and Lesotho, are home to a range of Proteaceae which occupy a variety of habitats. As is the case farther north with the tropical species, none is found in dry areas such as the Kalahari, Bushmanland and the Great Karoo. In regions of higher rainfall, they are missing from the Lowveld as well as Maputaland.

In South Africa, *Protea caffra* is represented by the subspecies *caffra* which, like the tropical subspecies, is a common and widespread plant, often forming a protea savannah on the high- and mid-altitude grasslands of the Highveld, Mpumalanga and KwaZulu-Natal. These grasslands are also the habitat of *P. roupelliae* ssp. *roupelliae*, a similarly wide-ranging, frequently encountered species.

*Protea nubigena* and *P. laetans* are both rare and highly localized. *Protea nubigena* is known only from a single group of about 50 plants which cling to a grassy, near-vertical south-facing slope on Policeman's Helmet ridge below the Amphitheatre in the KwaZulu-Natal Drakensberg – an extraordinary habitat for a protea as the slope is shaded most of the time and frozen over for long periods in winter. *P. laetans* grows on mountain slopes overlooking the Blyde River Canyon in Mpumalanga.

*Leucospermum gerrardii* is a low-growing shrub found on sandstone outcrops in the midlands of KwaZulu-Natal, where it is rare, and among quartzite and granite rocks high in the mountains above Barberton and Nelspruit as well as in eastern Swaziland.

*Protea caffra* ssp. *caffra* in the KwaZulu-Natal Drakensberg

*Protea roupelliae* ssp. *roupelliae*

*Protea laetans*

*Protea nubigena*

*Leucospermum gerrardii*

*Protea dracomontana*

*Protea dracomontana* grows along the Eastern Cape and KwaZulu-Natal escarpment but only in soils derived from basalt rock. *Protea simplex* is also occasionally encountered at lower altitudes both here and in the Mpumalanga mountains, but is also found on suitable rocky sites extending down to the KwaZulu-Natal coast. *Protea dracomontana* and *P. simplex* cope with being burnt off in the frequent, in places annual, fires in their grassland habitats by resprouting from an underground rootstock. Other subtropical proteas have evolved different strategies: the thick bark of tree species such as *P. roupelliae* and *P. caffra*, for instance, protects them from all but the hottest burns.

Fire has been a part of this and similar environments throughout Africa for a very long time but it is only in the past few thousand years, with the arrival of pastoralist peoples, that it has been as frequent. In these areas in their pristine state, before their modification by humans, grasslands were less extensive than they are today; certainly the forests were larger and the fynbos plant communities, which now cling to tiny patches of shallow soil, probably more widespread.

*Protea comptonii,* a tree with a spreading crown, can reach 8 m in height. Only two populations are known, one in the mountains above Barberton in Mpumalanga, the other on Louwsberg, which looms above the Itala Game Reserve in northern KwaZulu-Natal. *Protea curvata* is also rare: it is confined to a very small area north of Barberton, growing in bushveld on an unusual, geologically very ancient rock formation.

*Protea comptonii*

*Protea simplex*

*Protea curvata*

# PONDOLAND

Along the southern KwaZulu-Natal and Transkei coasts is an area which has a large number of endemic plants, many of them with obvious links to the Cape fynbos. In this Pondoland Centre, a rock very like the Table Mountain sandstone of the Cape fold mountains outcrops in places. The very rare *Raspalia trigyna*, for example, a species of the otherwise endemic Cape fynbos family Bruniaceae, grows in this habitat. Several summer rainfall species of *Protea* are found here but, of greater interest, are the Proteaceae which are Pondoland endemics.

*Leucospermum innovans* is one, a rare plant confined to just a few small populations on the edge of sandstone krantzes and threatened by the expansion of sugar and tea plantations. Another is the recently discovered *Leucadendron pondoense*, whose future looks more secure because several of the streams in which it grows run through proclaimed nature reserves. *Leucadendron spissifolium* is a plant which also grows – in the form of its subspecies *spissifolium*, *phillipsii* and *fragrans* – in suitable habitats throughout the Cape fynbos; the remaining two subspecies, *natalense* and *oribinum*, are found in the Pondoland Centre.

Why are there plants here with obvious Cape affinities? An intriguing, but unsubstantiated, suggestion is that when sea levels were much lower than they are now, suitable rock formations were exposed which may have provided a link to this area from the fynbos of the eastern Cape. Their subsequent inundation isolated the ancestors of the present-day Pondoland Centre Proteaceae.

*Leucadendron spissifolium* ssp. *natalense* on the KwaZulu-Natal coast

*Leucadendron pondoense* (female)

74

*Leucadendron pondoense* (male)

*Leucadendron spissifolium* spp. *oribinum* (male)

*Leucadendron spissifolium* spp. *oribinum* (female)

*Leucospermum innovans*

75

*Leucospermum cuneiforme* in grassy fynbos

In the west, the Cape Floral Region is isolated from the African savanna and grasslands by the arid areas of Namaqualand and the Great Karoo. The eastern Cape, however, is the meeting place, (the only one), of the Cape fynbos and the Succulent Karoo vegetation on the one hand, and the dominant vegetation types of the rest of sub-Saharan Africa on the other. Thus it is not surprising that, around the eastern end of the Cape Floral Region, the distinctions between different veld types become a little blurred. Very recently a single, small population of the KwaZulu-Natal Drakensberg species *Protea subvestita* was found in the Swartberg mountains, providing an intriguing link between fynbos and high-altitude grassland.

In the eastern Cape there is a type of fynbos, called grassy fynbos, in which grasses rather than Cape reeds (Restionaceae) are the dominant understorey plants. Part of this area also has its own, unique valley bushveld vegetation from which Proteaceae are entirely absent, probably because it is too dry. Neighbouring grassy fynbos areas, however, are home to several Proteaceae, among them *Protea lorifolia*, *Leucospermum cuneiforme* and the ubiquitous *Leucadendron salignum,* all of which are at the eastern extension of their distribution ranges here.

*Protea foliosa* grows on quartzite rocks on the hills around Riebeek East and Grahamstown, an area of mainly summer rainfall, and on Table Mountain sandstone near Port Elizabeth, where rainfall is spread more evenly through the year. *Leucadendron spissifolium* ssp. *phillipsii* is found both in the Van Stadens mountains near Port Elizabeth and in the Tsitsikamma mountains of the southern Cape.

*Leucadendron spissifolium* ssp. *phillipsii* (male)

*Protea lorifolia*

*Protea foliosa*

*Protea subvestita* in the Swartberg

# THE SOUTHERN COASTAL MOUNTAINS

The scenic backdrop to the southern Cape's Garden Route is a long, seemingly unbroken range of mountains. From as far west as Montagu, the Langeberg, Attaquaskloof and Outeniqua mountains separate the coastal strip from an arid valley, the Little Karoo, to the north. Farther eastwards, essentially the same range continues as the Tsitsikammas.

These mountains receive a lot of rain – from the cold fronts which sweep across the Cape in winter and spring, but also from the southwards extension of tropical summer weather systems. As a result, their southern slopes and the adjoining coastal plateau carry an exceptionally dense, tall fynbos, together with the forests for which the area is famous. This type of fynbos is the home of *Mimetes pauciflorus* (an Outeniquas and Tsitsikammas endemic), so named because the clusters of flowers on the flowerhead comprise just three or four flowers each. One of the most striking of the large-flowered pincushions, *Leucospermum glabrum*, also grows in this habitat.

The northern slopes of the range become progressively drier as they drop down to the Little Karoo. In renosterveld, on the very edge of this dry valley, grows *Leucospermum pluridens*, the vicariant of *L. glabrum*. *Leucospermum mundii* is another lovely pincushion found in small, isolated groups in the fynbos of the Langeberg farther west. *Protea coronata* is common along the low south slopes of the Attaquaskloof and Outeniquas. It is also plentiful on the coastal plateau to the east.

*Leucospermum mundii*

*Mimetes pauciflorus* in the Outeniquas

*Leucospermum glabrum*

*Protea coronata*

Standing high between the Little and Great Karoos, and running parallel to the coastal mountains to the south, lies the Swartberg range. These inland mountains receive less rainfall than their southern counterparts and, because they are far from the sea, they experience extremes of weather. Summers are hot and mostly dry, so the plants here have to endure long periods of desiccation. In winter, snowfalls are frequent and, on the high ground, the soil can remain frozen for weeks.

Swartberg plants are uniquely adapted to these harsh conditions. In the Proteaceae, two of the local specials are *Protea aristata* and *P. venusta*. The former is found only on the Klein Swartberg near Ladismith; *Protea venusta*, although rare, is encountered as scattered plants at high altitudes over the much greater area of the Groot

Swartberg and the Kammanassies. This species is related to *P. punctata*, which is common on these mountains, and occasionally you can find natural hybrids of the two. *Leucospermum secundifolium* is another rare plant, known only from the mountains around Ladismith. Its tiny flowerheads, along the ends of stems which trail along the ground, are atypical of the genus *Leucospermum*.

*Leucadendron album* grows in large, dense colonies on the mid slopes of the Swartberg and the massed effect of its silvery foliage is spectacular. Another shrub, beautiful, because of its large, colourful flowerheads, is *Leucadendron pubibracteolatum*. Related to this species and equally impressive in flower is *L. barkerae*, which occupies the desiccated low northern slopes on the edge of the Great Karoo.

*Leucadendron pubibracteolatum* (male)

*Leucadendron album* (male)

*Leucadendron barkerae* on the north side of the Swartberg

*Protea aristata*

*Leucospermum secundifolium*

*Protea venusta*

81

The tops of mountains are inhospitable places for plants and animals alike: sunlight and ultraviolet radiation are intense; the wind blows most of the time and seldom gently; ambient temperatures swing rapidly between extremes. Although the Cape mountains are not particularly high compared with some of those elsewhere in Africa, the plants that live on their peaks are specially adapted to the harsh conditions there.

Perhaps the best known of the subalpine Proteaceae is the snow protea *Protea cryophila*. Its specific name means 'lover of cold', and this it would certainly have to be as its home is the highest peaks of the Cederberg, which are covered with snow for long periods in winter. Little known is the snow protea's sister species, *P. pruinosa*, which occupies an equally harsh habitat high in the Swartberg mountains. 'Pruinosa' means 'frosted', a deliberately ambiguous reference both to the species habitat and to the white fur which covers the outside of the plant's bracts (like that of *P. cryophila*).

*Leucadendron dregei*, a small shrub that sprawls over the rocks on the summits of the Swartberg, is a rare species which, like many of the long-lived, slow-growing woody plants that grow on these and other high Cape mountains, is getting rarer as they are burnt by too-frequent, man-made fires.

The Langeberg range is exceptionally rich in endemic plants. Two of its endemic Proteaceae are *Spatalla nubicola* and *Leucadendron radiatum*. Both of these lovely species are rare and both are found only at the very top of the Langeberg's highest peaks.

*Leucadendron dregei* (male)

*Protea pruinosa*

*Spatalla nubicola*

*Leucadendron radiatum* (male)

# LIMESTONE SPECIES

Along the Cape south coast, between the Gouritz River mouth in the east and Gansbaai near Hermanus in the west, lies a series of low limestone hills, some overlooking the sea, some set a kilometre or two inland. These are the home of a specially adapted endemic flora which includes several interesting Proteaceae.

A few million years ago, sea levels around the Cape were higher than they are today. The sea floor next to the coast of that time, full of the shells of marine organisms, was later exposed as sea levels dropped. Rain partially dissolved the shells, in the process cementing them together to form limestone rock known as the Bredasdorp Formation. The exposure of this substrate created a new habitat which was colonized by plants from older surrounding areas. In adapting to the new conditions there, the plants changed through the process of natural selection and became new species.

*Mimetes saxatilis*, one of these limestone endemics, is related to the silver mimetes (see page 52) but, with the best will in the world, cannot be compared with these for beauty. More impressive is another limestone species, *Leucadendron meridianum*, a large bush whose uppermost leaves turn a spectacular silvery-yellow when it flowers. By contrast *L. muirii*, another limestone leucadendron, is an ugly duckling. Two other prominent Proteaceae found only on this rock type are *Protea obtusifolia*, and *Leucospermum truncatum*. The latter varies considerably along the length of the Bredasdorp Formation and is probably a species in the process of separating into different forms which may in time become distinct species.

*Mimetes saxatilis*

*Protea obtusifolia*

*Leucadendron meridianum* on coastal limestone hills

*Leucadendron muirii* (male)

*Leucospermum truncatum*

85

*Leucadendron modestum* (male)

*Protea pudens*

The small-flowered form of *Protea longifolia*

The extent of the Agulhas Plain has varied enormously over the past two million years or so, as sea levels have dropped and risen again in concert with the periodic expansion and contraction of the polar ice-caps. At times the coastline was more than 100 km farther south than it is today; at others the plain was almost completely inundated. The area's plants have had to adapt to a changing environment and, in the process, new species have evolved. In some parts, an unusual, shallow, gravelly soil has been exposed and here grows a collection of equally unusual plants in what is called Elim fynbos, named after the well-known mission town nearby.

*Protea longifolia* is fairly widespread in the southwestern Cape, but the Elim fynbos form has small, delicate flowerheads and looks somewhat like *Protea pudens*, an Elim fynbos endemic. 'Pudens' means 'shy', which aptly describes the way the flowerheads of this lovely species are held, facing down or sideways, on the ends of the branches. *Leucadendron modestum* is just one of several leucadendrons which are endemic to this vegetation, while *Leucospermum heterophyllum* is the only pincushion that is endemic.

Elim fynbos, like other vegetation types on the Agulhas Plain, is under huge threat from the invasive alien acacias, which now cover large areas on the plain, and from the expansion of the farmlands. The establishment of the Agulhas National Park, now in progress, will go a long way in conserving this unique lowland vegetation.

*Leucospermum heterophyllum*

*Leucadendron gandogeri* in the Kleinrivier mountains

Potberg is a Table Mountain sandstone ridge which stands at the eastern end of the De Hoop Nature Reserve, above the western bank of the Breede River just before it reaches the sea. It lies far from similar geological formations, such as the Bredasdorp and Kleinrivier mountains to the west and the Riviersonderend and Langeberg ranges inland, and, as a result of its long isolation, it supports many plants which are not found anywhere else. *Protea aurea*, very common on the coastal side of the southern Cape mountains and also found on the Riviersonderend range, has smooth leaves. On Potberg, there is the only known population of this species with very broad, hairy leaves and this is described as the subspecies *potbergensis*. *Protea denticulata* is found only on Potberg.

*Leucospermum gracile* is confined to the sea-facing slopes of the Bredasdorp mountains and the Kleinrivier mountains near Hermanus farther west.

Inland is the Riviersonderend range, on whose northern slopes occurs the rare species *Leucadendron burchellii*. These mountains are at the eastern edge of the predominantly winter-rainfall southwestern Cape region. Farther eastwards, the land receives increasing amounts of summer rain.

There is no doubt that summer aridity was important in shaping the evolution of the Cape flora, but the fynbos of the southern Cape mountains provides ample proof that this vegetation type thrives in areas where rainfall is not restricted to the winter months.

*Protea aurea* ssp. *potbergensis*

*Leucadendron burchellii* (female)

*Leucospermum gracile*

*Protea denticulata*

89

*Protea stokoei*

*Spatalla mollis*

A relief map of the Cape shows that the mountains at the southern tip of Africa form a giant 'L', the foot of the letter representing the southern Cape mountains, the back of the letter representing the Tulbagh, Kouebokkeveld and Cederberg ranges in the west. It is no accident that these two series of ranges run more or less parallel to the nearest coast: they mark the lines along which unimaginably huge forces tore this part of the ancient continent, or supercontinent, of Gondwana apart and gave the Cape its present day form. If you stand on the top of Cape Town's Table Mountain and look to your north, you will see part of the great complex of mountains, which is where these two groups of ranges meet.

The southwestern Cape is the heart of the Cape flora, and on these mountains you will find the richest, most varied fynbos – the dominant vegetation of the Cape flora and the component which makes that unique. This is as true for the Proteaceae as it is for the fynbos as a whole: the southwestern Cape mountains are at the core of the distribution ranges of all the genera of the African Proteaceae except *Faurea* and, technically, *Vexatorella*. They are also home to many gems of the family. The queen protea *Protea magnifica*, *P. stokoei* and the mountain rose *P. nana*, illustrate some of the variety of proteas here. *Leucospermum tottum* is a species used in programmes to produce cultivars for the cut-flower trade. *Spatalla mollis* represents one of the little known, smaller genera.

*Protea nana*

*Protea magnifica*

*Leucospermum tottum*

*Leucadendron xanthoconus* is one of the leucadendrons which grow in dense colonies that turn mountainsides brilliant yellow when they flower in spring. In no one place is this a permanent feature of the landscape: these plants are a part of the shrubby component of the fynbos which is burnt off in the recurring fires that are an inherent part of their environment. They regenerate from seed, retained in the cones of mature female plants until the next fire comes along. It takes several years before the new plants are mature enough to flower and repeat the show.

Unlike *Leucadendron xanthoconus*, the cones of *L. sessile* drop their seeds when they are ripe. Although this species grows in colonies, and the flowering plants are individually colourful, it does not produce such massed displays of colour. At the other extreme of the showiness spectrum is *Leucospermum cordatum*. This small, extremely rare and localized species is difficult to find among the restios on the steep mountain slope above Kogel Bay which is its only known home.

*Protea scabra*, another cryptic species, is one of the dwarf proteas with underground stems that send up tufts of narrow leaves. The flowers grow at the base of the tufts. This species' response to fire is very different from that of the shrubby Proteaceae: after a burn, its underground branches, stimulated by the heat and a sudden rush of nutrients in the form of ash, simply grow another lot of leaf tufts. *Protea scabra* and similar proteas flower most prolifically in the season after a fire. Thereafter they suffer increasing competition from the taller growing shrubs.

*Leucospermum cordatum*

*Protea scabra*

*Leucadendron sessile* (male)

*Leucadendron xanthoconus* in the Kogelberg

The word 'peninsula' comes from two Latin words which translate as 'almost an island'. This most famous of the Cape's mountain ranges is just that. In fact, during the past million or two years it has sometimes – when high sea levels have periodically inundated the Cape Flats – truly been an island. As such it has, to a certain degree, been isolated from the rest of the southwestern Cape. This separation is reflected in the large number of its endemics – plant species that are found here but not on the 'mainland'.

One subspecies of the kreupelhout, *Leucospermum conocarpodendron* ssp. *viridum*, has a fairly wide distribution in the southwestern Cape, growing on a variety of soil types. The other, ssp. *conocarpodendron*, is found only on the Peninsula, on soils derived from Cape granite. *Serruria collina* and *S. glomerata* are two of the Peninsula's six endemic serrurias; *Leucadendron strobilinum* one of its three endemic leucadendrons. *Protea speciosa*, however, grows here as well as in suitable habitats over a large part of the southwestern Cape.

The Peninsula has an extremely rich and varied flora that includes more than 2 600 species of flowering plants. Many of these are rare, some naturally so but others victims of the intense pressures imposed by a burgeoning human population. The historic proclamation of the Cape Peninsula National Park has launched a concerted and co-ordinated drive to conserve the remaining natural areas of the Peninsula and, with them, the habitats of a large proportion of its indigenous plants, including most of its endemic Proteaceae.

*Serruria collina*

*Protea speciosa*

*Serruria glomerata*

*Leucadendron strobilinum* (male)

*Leucospermum conocarpodendron* ssp. *conocarpodendron* above Camps Bay

*Leucadendron daphnoides* (female)

*Leucospermum gueinzii*

Silver trees *Leucadendron argenteum* on Cape Town's Lion's Head

The female inflorescence of the silver tree *Leucadendron argenteum*

Cape granite is a very ancient rock, formed some 500 to 600 million years ago, long before the Table Mountain sandstone of the Cape Fold Mountains. Today, granite boulders, with their unmistakable rounded shapes, are still visible in the southwestern Cape.

The best known of these outcrops are those on the Atlantic side of the Peninsula, around the Langebaan Lagoon in the West Coast National Park, and Paarl Rock, which overlooks the Winelands town of that name. The soil formed by the granite's weathering is different from the more widespread sands and clays of the southwestern Cape.

Several species of Proteaceae are confined to granite. *Leucadendron argenteum*, the silver tree, is the most famous of these. This species is native to the northern part of the Cape Peninsula, Paarl Mountain, Tygerberg,

Simonsberg and the Helderberg, and its beautiful reflective leaves have made it a much valued ornamental. A quick-growing, short-lived tree seldom surviving longer than 60 years, it served as an important source of fuel and rough building timber in the days of the early Dutch colonists at the Cape who also fed its large, nutritious, nut-like seeds to their poultry.

*Leucospermum gueinzii* grows on granitic soils in the Jonkershoek valley near Stellenbosch, and also on the Helderberg to the south. *Leucadendron daphnoides* is found in large groups on mountain slopes between the northern side of the Du Toit's Kloof Pass and Villiersdorp to the southeast, but only where there are granite outcrops. The species is spectacular in flower, when the leaves around the flowerheads are coloured ivory, turning dull red as the flowers age.

# PROTEACEAE IN RENOSTERVELD

Renosterveld is one of the minor vegetation types of the Cape flora. Taking its name from the renosterbos (*Elytropappus rhinocerotis*), its dominant plant, renosterveld grows on shale soils. In the south-west these are the Malmesbury shales, the most ancient of the exposed rocks in the southwestern Cape, now covered with the wheatfields of the Swartland. Elsewhere in the Cape Floral Region, they are the Bokkeveld shales, part of the same group of rock formations as Table Mountain sandstone. Renosterveld grows on these soils where rainfall is moderate; fynbos is found on these substrates but only if the annual precipitation is high. The dry areas of these soils carry Succulent Karoo vegetation. Because the shale soils are the richest in the southwestern Cape, the renosterveld areas have been massively transformed by agriculture and most of the renosterveld Proteaceae are becoming increasingly rare. Only a few Proteaceae species, however, grow naturally in renosterveld, and none is part of Succulent Karoo vegetation. Of the proteas, *Protea odorata*, with its tiny flowerheads, and its sister species, *P. mucronifolia*, are perhaps the most interesting; *Leucadendron verticillatum* is an attractive plant, with silvery foliage. The only viable population of this species is within the private Eensaamheid reserve north of Durbanville. Here can also be found *Serruria pinnata* (another threatened plant), which is very like the montane species *S. gracilis*. *Serruria brownii*, once common, is now considered vulnerable because farming is destroying its habitat. Equally at risk, and for the same reason, is *Protea restionifolia*, which grows on the margins of fynbos, where this vegetation grades into renosterveld or Succulent Karoo vegetation. This protea is another of the dwarf plants which produce their flowerheads at ground level and is almost certainly pollinated by rodents.

*Leucadendron verticillatum* (male)

*Serruria brownii*

*Protea restionifolia*

*Serruria pinnata*

Few Proteaceae like to stand with their roots in water and none is found on permanently waterlogged ground. However, several species grow in wet situations, most notably the plants that occupy peaty slopes high on the coastal mountains of the southwestern and southern Cape. The soil here is little more than decomposed plant matter, and is kept permanently moist by the clouds which bring moisture from the nearby sea in the form of mist. This is the unique habitat of the famous marsh rose *Orothamnus zeyheri,* as well as of the spectacularly lovely *Mimetes hottentoticus.*

At lower elevations, a number of species grow in seeps where water run-off from surrounding slopes maintains high soil moisture. *Leucadendron spissifolium* ssp. *spissifolium,* widespread in the southwestern Cape, is one such. Another is *Mimetes hirtus,* which grows virtually at sea level – in the Cape of Good Hope reserve and near Betty's Bay – but also at high altitudes in the Kleinrivier mountains near Hermanus. The common factor in these disparate environments is their high soil moisture level. *Diastella parilis,* a rare plant becoming even rarer as its limited habitat shrinks with the expansion of agriculture, occurs in seeps at the foot of the mountains in the Breede River valley near Slanghoek.

*Leucadendron conicum,* like the wild almond *Brabejum stellatifolium,* grows in another type of moist habitat – next to rivers and streams in the southern Cape mountains – where it can become a sizeable tree.

*Mimetes hirtus* in the Cape of Good Hope reserve

*Leucadendron spissifolium* ssp. *spissifolium* (female)

*Leucadendron conicum*

*Diastella parilis*

*Leucospermum spathulatum*

*Leucadendron loranthifolium* (male)

*Leucospermum vestitum*

The rare yellow form of *Leucospermum reflexum*

The rocket pincushion *Leucospermum reflexum*

The mountain ranges which run northwards from the southwestern Cape towns of Ceres and Tulbagh stretch towards Namaqualand, one of southern Africa's deserts. To their east is the little-known Tanqua Karoo, a long valley of equally daunting aridity which separates the ranges from the Roggeveld escarpment. Because they lie fairly far from the coast to the west, the climate here is not greatly tempered by the Atlantic's cold seas. This is a part of the Cape Floral Region that truly experiences summer drought, and many of its plants are specially adapted and live naturally nowhere else.

There are no Proteaceae on the Roggeveld escarpment, and certainly none in the Tanqua, but the Tulbagh, Kouebokkeveld and Cederberg mountains are home to a fascinating range of species from this family.

Some of the variety of the Proteaceae species found here are illustrated on these pages. Chief among these must be the snow protea *Protea cryophila*, found only on the highest peaks of the Cederberg, above the winter snowline. Attempts to grow this extraordinary plant at lower altitudes in more moderate climates have failed. Another of the Cederberg's specials, however, is well known (and loved ) in cultivation: the rocket pincushion *Leucospermum reflexum* grows naturally at much lower altitudes. The common form of this species has flower-heads of a dusky orange colour, but a form with clear yellow flowers is extensively grown. The latter form is very rare in nature – only two such plants are currently known in the whole of the Cederberg Wilderness Area, which is the species' only natural home.

*Protea witzenbergiana*

*Leucadendron glaberrimum* ssp. *erubescens* (female)

*Leucadendron gydoense* (female)

*Sorocephalus lanatus*

The snow protea *Protea cryophila*

Dunefields are a feature of much of the southern African coastline. In the Cape, the sandy beaches of several millions of years ago, when sea levels were much higher than they are now, were left literally high and dry when the ocean later retreated. The action of wind and fluctuating, albeit lower, sea-levels during the last one or two million years has formed them into the dunes we see today. In addition, wind has spread the sand over huge areas of adjoining coastal plain and, where mountains abut the dunes, even pushed plumes of sand high up their slopes. Such plumes are clearly evident near Betty's Bay in the southwestern Cape and above Hout Bay on the Cape Peninsula.

A variety of Proteaceae have colonized these geologically recent sands. One of these is *Protea scolymocephala*, a widespread species found from the Gifberg, north of the Cederberg, all the way south to the Peninsula. The sprawling pincushion *Leucospermum prostratum* grows on dunes and sand flats eastwards along the coast from Betty's Bay, and also on the low Table Mountain sandstone hills just inland. A related, equally prostrate species, *Leucospermum pedunculatum*, is rare and found only close to the sea in deep sand on the Agulhas Plain. The former may be an older species that was capable of colonizing the coastal sands when they were exposed; the latter is clearly a recently evolved species. *Diastella proteoides*, once common in sandveld fynbos areas north and east of Cape Town, is now rare; most of its habitat has been transformed or overrun by alien Australian acacias which are particularly well-suited to these sands.

*Protea scolymocephala*

*Leucospermum prostratum* on coastal dunes

*Diastella proteoides*

*Leucospermum pedunculatum*

*Protea sulphurea*

*Leucospermum rodolentum*

*Protea namaquana*

The Protea family does not seem to have had the genetic potential which other Cape families, such as the Mesembryanthemaceae, the succulent vygies, have harnessed in adapting to very arid regions. Its extension northwards from the Cape has apparently been blocked by the very dry parts of Namaqualand and by the Great Karoo. Nevertheless, Proteaceae are found in some marginal habitats bordering these no-go areas.

*Protea sulphurea*, one of the loveliest of all proteas, grows on the sun-baked, north-facing slopes of the Montagu, Witteberg and Swartberg mountains, where Table Mountain sandstone meets the shale soils of the Karoo. The species is perfectly adapted to the harsh climate of its habitat and, because of the infrequent fires here, can live for decades.

Few people are aware that the sandveld fynbos of the Cape West Coast extends far northwards well into Namaqualand. Botanists have only recently explored and studied Namaqualand's coastal plain in detail, and the huge extent of this vegetation type has come as a great surprise. *Leucospermum rodolentum* and *L. praemorsum* are two hardy pincushions which form part of the shrubby component of Namaqualand's sandveld fynbos.

Namaqualand is also home to another type of fynbos. Growing on the very highest peaks of the granitic Kamiesberg mountains are ericas, restios and a host of other typically fynbos plants, including just two Proteaceae species. One of these is *Vexatorella alpina*, which grows into a large shrub and is locally very common; the other is *Protea namaquana*, which looks somewhat like *P. sulphurea* and is probably related (though it is clear that populations of the two species have been separated for a very long time).

*Leucospermum praemorsum* on inland dunes near Hondeklip Bay

Male flowerheads of *Leucadendron rubrum*

Scarab beetles on *Protea welwitschii*

Plants interact with animals, including birds and insects, in a variety of ways. Some of the most fascinating of these are involved in the all-important process of reproduction. For most plants, and this includes all of the Proteaceae, reproduction requires the transfer of pollen from one flower to another. This requires the services of an external agent because plants cannot move purposefully to do it themselves. A few Proteaceae simply produce a lot of pollen and rely on the wind to move it between plants; *Leucadendron rubrum* is one of them. The rest rely on the services of an animal to take pollen from one flowerhead to another. Despite our fascination with them, plants do not produce flowers to please humans but to attract pollinators. The form and colour of flowers have been ruthlessly selected over long periods of time because the genes of a sexually repro-ducing plant which does not attract pollinators, die with it.

Insects appeared on earth long before flowering plants, so it is not surprising that they played a pivotal role in the evolution of the latter. Today, they are the main pollinators of most of southern Africa's Proteaceae.

The most important of them are the beetles (particularly protea scarab beetles and monkey beetles in the family Scarabaeidae), flies, wasps and a variety of bees, including the honey bee *Apis mellifera*.

It has long been suspected that nocturnal moths could play a role in the pollination of a number of scented, pale-flowered species, but the photograph here (opposite page, above right) is the first documentary evidence that this may be the case.

As far as is known, ants play no part in the pollination of the southern African Proteaceae but, in the case of many of the genera, they serve as important agents for the dispersal and storage of seeds.

The seeds of *Leucospermum*, *Vexatorella*, *Diastella*, *Serruria*, *Paranomus*, *Spatalla*, *Sorocephalus* and *Orothamnus* species carry a fleshy appendage which is attractive to certain kinds of fynbos ants. In a process known as myrmecochory, the ants collect these seeds and store them underground, where they are safe from predation by birds and rodents, and where they can germinate after the passing of a fire.

A honey bee *Apis mellifera* working *Serruria villosa*

A noctuid moth *Cytothymia* sp. on *Serruria adscendens*

Monkey beetles *Anisonyx ursus* on *Leucadendron burchellii*

Pugnacious ants carrying off a seed of *Mimetes cucullatus*

111

# POLLINATION BY BIRDS

Throughout the family's southern hemisphere distribution birds are important pollinators of many of the species of Proteaceae with large flowerheads. In southern Africa, however, only the genus *Mimetes* has evolved flowerheads specially designed for bird pollination. In the southwestern and southern Cape, sunbirds – particularly the orangebreasted sunbird *Nectarinia violacea*, but also malachite sunbirds *Nectarinia famosa* and lesser doublecollared sunbirds *Nectarinia chalybea* – visit *Mimetes* species in flower. Cape sugarbirds *Promerops cafer* also pollinate species such as *M. hirtus* and *M. hottentoticus*.

Birds often visit the flowerheads of some proteas and pincushions but, equally, so do beetles. Cape sugarbirds are very active on proteas like *Protea neriifolia*, *Protea laurifolia* and *P. magnifica*, which have deep flowerheads. Sunbirds, with their shorter beaks, cannot reach into these and get to the nectar at the bottom of the flowerhead successfully. Sunbirds work those proteas with shorter or more wide-open flowerheads (*P. aurea* for example). Cape sugarbirds and sunbirds are important pollinators of many of the *Leucospermum* species that have large, yellow, orange or red flowerheads.

In the Cape Floral Region, Cape sugarbirds are seldom found far from the Proteaceae which provide their main source of food, although they do visit plants of other families (*Watsonia tabularis*, for example, on the Cape Peninsula). The sunbirds are far more versatile, taking nectar from many different flowers suited to bird pollination ranging from ericas to aloes.

On the Drakensberg mountains of the Eastern Cape province and KwaZulu-Natal, the role that the Cape sugarbird plays in the Cape flora is assumed by its vicariant, Gurney's sugarbird *Promerops gurneyi*, whose range is dictated by the distribution of such proteas as *P. roupelliae*, but which also visits other plants like aloes.

A male Cape sugarbird *Promerops cafer* in a *Leucospermum conocarpodendron* ssp. *conocarpodendron* flowerhead

A male Cape sugarbird *Promerops cafer* reaching inside the flowerhead of *Protea neriifolia*

A male orangebreasted sunbird *Nectarinia violacea*
on *Mimetes fimbrifolius*

A juvenile lesser doublecollared sunbird resting on
*Leucospermum cordifolium*

# POLLINATION BY RODENTS AND BUTTERFLIES

Other than *Mimetes*, only one group of southern African Proteaceae has evolved to attract a specific pollinator. The pollination of a group of proteas by rodents such as the ubiquitous striped mouse *Rhabdomys pumilio*, the Namaqua rock mouse *Aethomys namaquensis* and the pygmy mouse *Mus minutoides*, has been comprehensively studied and documented. The flowerheads of these *Protea* species, among them *P. humiflora*, *P. amplexicaulis* and *P. subulifolia*, are carried not at the ends of their branches but close to the ground, and they give off a yeasty smell. This attracts the rodents, which forage for nectar, in the process inadvertently collecting pollen on their heads, which is then brushed off when they visit another flowerhead. The rodents also eat bits of the flowerheads – the bracts, for instance – but this sacrifice by the plants would seem well worth their while since the positioning of their flowerheads is unlikely to attract birds, flying insects or other pollinators to them. Striped mice are sometimes active in the daylight and have been seen on *Protea* species, such as *P. neriifolia,* which do not belong to the group, but this behaviour seems incidental. The other mice are nocturnal. Rodents may also be active pollinators of other proteas, ones with open flowerheads such as *P. acuminata* and *P. sulphurea* and of two pincushions, *Leucospermum hamatum* and *L. harpagonatum*, but this has not been documented.

Butterflies have been recorded visiting some Proteaceae, such as *Paranomus bracteolaris* in the Cederberg, but they are not thought to be important pollinators of the Proteaceae. In the Baviaanskloof mountains, however, the Table Mountain pride butterfly *Aeropetes tulbaghia* has been repeatedly seen working the flowerheads of *Protea punctata*, in the process chasing off orangebreasted sunbirds. This is strange behaviour for an insect which, in the southwestern Cape and farther north in the summer rainfall area of South Africa, is associated with a suite of red or orange summer flowers which includes not a single Proteaceae. The explanation for this may be found in the temporary or local dearth of the flowers to which *Aeropetes* is more attracted.

The Table Mountain pride butterfly *Aeropetes tulbaghia* on *Protea punctata*

A Namaqua rock mouse *Aethomys namaquensis* with *Protea humiflora*

# FIRE AND REGENERATION

Southern African Proteaceae are found in a variety of vegetation types, ranging from savannah and grasslands to many different types of fynbos. Wherever they are found, though, the plant cover is prone to fire and burns repeatedly. The only possible exception to this is the sandveld fynbos of Namaqualand's coastal plain, which is indeed fire-prone but probably burns very seldom as it is surrounded by succulent vegetation that cannot sustain a fire. Many of the Proteaceae have evolved specialized features in response to fires.

Quite a number of Proteaceae have underground root-stocks which send up new stems after the aerial parts of the plants have been burnt or otherwise destroyed. *Leucadendron spissifolium* is a typical example of this.

Such a capacity for regeneration has allowed several of the summer-rainfall proteas and pincushions to survive in grasslands that are burnt annually by livestock farmers to provide new grass for grazing. In the Cape flora there are dwarf *Protea* species, with underground stems, which survive all but the hottest fires. Many of the tree-like proteas, pincushions and *Mimetes* species have thick bark which insulates the living tissue beneath; *Mimetes fimbrifolius*, for example, can produce new growth from leaf buds that are protected in this way.

When ants collect the myrmecochorous seeds of many of the Cape flora's Proteaceae and store them underground (see page 110), they are providing protection as much from fire as from seed-eating rodents, insects and birds. Another fire protection strategy, serotiny, which has been adopted by many of the Cape species of *Protea* and *Leucadendron* as well as two species of *Aulax*, involves the storage of seeds in a hard, woody cone which opens only after fire. The sugarbush *Protea repens*, and *P. laurifolia* are typical of the serotinous Protea species.

Regrowth on an old *Mimetes fimbrifolius* tree subjected to fire

*Leucadendron spissifolium* resprouting from its rootstock after fire

Fire in the fynbos

*Protea repens* flowerheads spilling seed after being burnt

Massed seedlings of *Protea laurifolia* under the burnt parent plant

117

*Serruria meisneriana*

*Serruria zeyheri*

*Sorocephalus tenuifolius*

*Leucadendron ericifolium*

The plants of the Cape have been collected and studied since the arrival of the first European visitors to this part of Africa. The first South African plant ever to have been illustrated in Europe was in fact a protea – *Protea neriifolia* – which had been collected at the Cape in 1597 by a Dutch trade mission on its way to Java. After the establishment of the Dutch East India Company settlement at the Cape in 1652, a few *Protea* species were among the many botanical curiosities which made their way to Europe.

Deliberate botanical exploration of the Cape flora began with the arrival at the Cape of Good Hope, in 1772, of Carl Thunberg, a student of the famous Swedish 'father of taxonomy', Linnaeus. Thunberg was the first of a succession of distinguished Europeans who came to the Cape during the following century to collect and study its extraordinary plants, men motivated by a varying mix of cupidity, curiosity, commercial acumen, scientific interest and derring-do.

Some of the herbarium records of these expeditions contained species which could not be found again, despite assiduous searches over many decades. Recently, however, a remarkable number of these missing plants have been traced, either as a result of intense exploration or, more often, through sheer luck. Among them are *Leucadendron ericifolium*, *Serruria meisneriana*, *S. zeyheri* and *S. roxburghii*.

About 17 years ago, the only site where *Sorocephalus tenuifolius* was known to grow was ploughed up. This was assumed to be the end of this rare species but, quite by chance, a large population has subsequently been found in a nearby nature reserve.

*Serruria roxburghii*

**119**

Willie Julies and *Mimetes chrysanthus*

*Mimetes chrysanthus*

*Serruria lacunosa*

*Leucadendron osbornei*

New species of plants continue to be discovered in southern Africa. This may seem amazing in view of the intense botanical exploration that has taken place since Europeans first settled on the subcontinent. One must bear in mind, however, the region's extraordinary diversity of plant life which, in turn, reflects the great variety of habitat. In the Cape, in particular, each mountain ridge may carry a set of plants that differs from its neighbour's. A glance through the window of an airliner flying over the Cape's mountains should be enough to show the observer that there are places down there which have probably never been walked, let alone by anyone with enough knowledge of plants to recognize a new species!

Over the past two decades alone, several new species of Proteaceae, previously neither collected nor described, have been discovered. The most sensational find was that of a new species of *Mimetes*. This was no tiny, insignificant herb with drab flowers, but a tall shrub,

prominent in the landscape, with brilliant yellow flowers. Why had it not been noted before? One reason is that *Mimetes chrysanthus* grows in dry fynbos on the south-facing slopes of Gamkaberg, and this low mountain in the middle of the Little Karoo had not, until very recently, been on the itineraries of plant collectors, old or modern. *M. chrysanthus* was discovered by Willie Julies, a game guard at the Gamka Mountain Nature Reserve, on the 7 September 1987. Since then, populations of this spectacular species have also turned up in arid fynbos on the northern foothills of the Outeniqua mountains.

*Leucadendron osbornei* is neither a rare plant nor diminutive, but a robust shrub which is fairly widespread on the very dry western end of the Klein Swartberg range. Yet it was discovered only in 1994. Its name commemorates its discoverer, Dave Osborne, then Nature Conservator for these mountains. It is related both to *L. nobile*, from the Baviaanskloof mountains, and the western Cape species *L. teretifolium*.

Elsie Esterhuysen, John Rourke and John Winter with *Vexatorella latebrosa*

The undescribed *Leucadendron* species: a remarkable plant that grows into a small tree with a massive trunk

In 1954 Elsie Esterhuysen, the legendary modern collector of Cape plants, collected a piece of a plant, which was past flowering, on the low south slopes of the Worcester mountains above Klaas Voogds near Robertson. It was 27 years later that the author joined her, John Rourke and John Winter of the National Botanical Institute, on a trip to locate and collect material for a thorough study. It had been clear from the first scraps found that the plant did not fit into any of the known Proteaceae genera. A detailed study led to the recognition of a new genus, *Vexatorella*. *Vexatorella latebrosa* is still known only from this one site.

The Protea Atlas Project is an initiative managed by the National Botanical Institute at Kirstenbosch. Its main aim is to stimulate popular interest in the flora of southern Africa by enlisting the help of interested people in mapping the details of the ranges of all the southern African Proteaceae. Protea Atlassers have also made several new discoveries. One of them is *Leucadendron osbornei* (see page 121). *Leucospermum harpagonatum*, an unusual sprawling pincushion from the Riviersonderend mountains above McGregor, is another. The three most recent such discoveries are *Serruria lacunosa* (see page 120), *Serruria rebeloi* (another small serruria, named after its discoverer, Tony Rebelo, who manages the Protea Atlas Project) and an as-yet unstudied *Leucadendron* species from the mountains above the Hex River Pass. The last, an extraordinary plant which grows into a small tree with a massive trunk, is most probably a new species.

The Cape is not the only area to yield new species of Proteaceae. *Leucadendron pondoense*, from the Transkei's Wild Coast, was described only in 1990.

*Serruria rebeloi*

*Leucospermum harpagonatum*

# ENVIRONMENTAL THREATS AND CONSERVATION

The threat posed to the continued existence of the southern African Proteaceae is, in essence, the same threat facing every single living thing on this planet, including humankind – the transformation and destruction, by human activity, of natural habitats. Evidence of what has been succinctly described as the sixth global extinction (the fifth saw the demise of the dinosaurs) is all around us. In August 1999, at the International Botanical Congress in St. Louis, Missouri, USA, the president, Peter Raven, dropped a bombshell. Extrapolating from current trends, he revealed that:
– one third of all the Earth's species of higher plants will have disappeared within 50 years;
– at the end of that period, just 5 per cent of the tropical forests will be left standing;
– less than one third of all the planet's current plant species will survive to the end of the 22nd century.

In southern Africa, there is a peculiar combination of socio-economic forces at work that poses a huge challenge to those striving to conserve pristine environments. The first comprises the actions of the aggressive, technologically sophisticated commercial, agricultural and industrial sectors. The second comprises the rapid increase in the number of people, the great majority of whom are relatively poor and unskilled but wanting a better life. The third comprises government's, preoccupation with improving the living conditions of its major constituency, the impoverished masses.

The enrichment of both the wealthy and the poorer, together or separately, morally or politically justified or not, inevitably derives from the consumption of natural resources and the transformation of natural areas. Government funds are concentrated in social projects, leaving little for environmental conservation.

Alien acacias in sandveld fynbos

What has this got to do with the Proteaceae? Everything! For example: huge areas of the mountains in the southern Cape, Eastern Cape, KwaZulu-Natal, Mpumalanga and the Eastern Highlands of Zimbabwe are already planted with exotic trees; aggressive afforestation of hitherto pristine areas is further reducing the natural ranges of the Proteaceae in these regions. In the Western Cape province, large areas of sandveld near Clanwilliam, until recently little affected by agriculture, are being cleared and planted to seed potatoes. Resort development and increasing urban sprawl around the South African coast are eliminating populations of several Proteaceae. Even conserved areas are not immune: at the time of writing, a devastating fire, started on a neighbouring farm, has cut a huge swathe through the recently proclaimed Kogelberg Biosphere Reserve, in the process burning large areas of veld only nine years old. Only heroic efforts by the fire-fighters kept the blaze out of even younger veld. Long-lived, slow-growing, localized species such as the rare *Mimetes arboreus* cannot survive too frequent fires

The future for the conservation of Proteaceae and other plant habitats in southern Africa is, however, not all doom and gloom. There are several encouraging factors. Many of the subcontinent's conserved areas are staffed by experienced, effective and committed people. Careful planning based on thorough research by organizations such as the Institute for Plant Conservation, at the University of Cape Town, has identified priority areas for conservation so that limited funding can be used to maximum effect. Money for the purchase of land is also being made available by local benefactors (among them the Leslie Hill Trust) and outside agencies (including the World Bank). Biological controls for some of the invasive alien plants, notably the Australian acacias and *Hakea* species, are proving effective. The South African government's Working for Water Programme has had an appreciable effect on these and other invader plants. Finally, private and government landowners are becoming more aware of the commercial potential for ecotourism, which is inextricably linked to the preservation of pristine environments and to the appreciation, here and abroad, of the subcontinent's unique plant life.

In the next few decades, several species of the Proteaceae, particularly lowland ones, may well be pushed by man into oblivion. Hopefully, the rest will survive as a result of the growing awareness, by the southern African public at large, of the absolute need to conserve what remains of the natural world here.

A massed infestation of the alien *Hakea gibbosa* behind *Aulax umbellata*

# USEFUL SOURCES

If you would like to find out more about the southern African Proteaceae, make a note of:

- *SASOL Proteas – A Field Guide to the Proteas of Southern Africa* by Tony Rebelo, published by Fernwood Press, Cape Town (1995), which illustrates and provides concise descriptions of all the family's species known, at that time, to occur on the subcontinent; an up-to-date edition may be released.
- The Protea Atlas Project is due to run until the end of 2001. If you are interested in learning about the Proteaceae in the field, and enjoying the process, you are most welcome to participate. For more information, contact the Co-ordinator, Val Charlton, Tel. South Africa (021) 7611425, email Protea@nbict.nbi.ac.za, or visit the Atlas's website, http://www.nbi.ac.za/protea/
- *The Proteas of Tropical Africa* by J. S. Beard, published by Kangaroo Press, the only popular account of the tropical species of *Protea*. This well-illustrated volume includes the only pincushion which reaches the tropics (*Leucospermum saxosum*), but covers none of the tropical *Faurea* species. The taxonomic concepts in the book differ somewhat from those of the SASOL guide (see above) and the titles recommended below.
- *The Proteas of Southern Africa* by J. P. Rourke, published by Purnell (1980): an equally beautifully illustrated

popular account of the southern African species of the genus Protea.

**Books about the Cape Flora include:**
- *The Cape Floral Kingdom* by Colin Paterson-Jones, Struik (1997): a beautifully illustrated showcase for the unique and lovely flowers of the Cape.
- *Fynbos – South Africa's Unique Floral Kingdom* by Richard Cowling and Dave Richardson, Fernwood Press (1995): a profusely illustrated and authoritative account of the Cape Flora.

**Books about the flowers of other southern African regions include:**
- *Namaqualand – A Succulent Desert* by Richard Cowling and Shirley Pierce, Fernwood Press (1999): a splendid companion volume to *Fynbos – South Africa's Unique Floral Kingdom*.
- A range of well-illustrated field guides to the flowering plants and trees of many of the subcontinent's regions, as well as a number of beautifully illustrated specialist monographs on some of the spectacular genera. For more information about these, contact The Botanical Society of South Africa, Tel. South Africa 021-7972090, or visit the society's website, http//:www.botsocsa.org.za/

# INDEX

# INDEX

Struik Publishers (Pty) Ltd
(a member of The Struik New Holland Publishing Group (Pty) Ltd)
Cornelis Struik House
80 McKenzie Street
Cape Town 8001

Reg No. 54/00965/07

First published 2000

1 3 5 7 9 10 8 6 4 2

Publishing manager: Pippa Parker, Managing editor: Simon Pooley
Editor: Peter Joyce, Editorial assitant: Giséle Raad,
Designer: Dominic Robson, Proofreader: Gill Gordon

Reproduction by Hirt & Carter (Pty) Ltd, Cape Town
Printed and bound by Kyodo Printing Co (Pte) Ltd, Singapore.

ISBN 1 86872 306 2

**The author gratefully acknowledges the contribution of
Dr John Rourke of the National Botanical Institute's
Compton Herbarium, Kirstenbosch, Cape Town, in
developing the concept for this book.**

Cover illustrations: Front cover: *Protea cynaroides*;
back cover: *Protea effusa* (top left); *Leucadendron bonum*
(female)(top right); *Leucadendron nervosum* (male) (bottom).